Published in the UK by Alison Green Books, 2025
An imprint of Scholastic
Bosworth Avenue, Warwick, CV34 6UQ
www.scholastic.co.uk

For safety or quality concerns:
UK: www.scholastic.co.uk/productinformation
EU: www.scholastic.ie/productinformation

Text © Julia Donaldson, 2007, 2008, 2011, 2017, 2025
Cover and inside illustrations © Axel Scheffler, 2007, 2008, 2011, 2017, 2025
Activities created by Little Wild Things © Julia Donaldson, 2025
Based on the bestselling picture books *Tiddler, Stick Man, The Highway Rat* and *The Ugly Five*

The moral rights of Julia Donaldson and Axel Scheffler have been asserted by them.

ISBN 978 0702 34179 3

A CIP catalogue record for this book is available from the British Library.

All rights reserved.
No part of this publication may be used to train any artificial intelligence technologies. Subject to EU law Scholastic Limited expressly reserves this work from the text and data mining exception.

Printed in China
Paper made from wood grown in sustainable forests and other controlled sources.

10 9 8 7 6 5 4 3 2 1

SCHOLASTIC and associated logos are trademarks and/or registered trademarks of Scholastic Inc.

STICK MAN
AND FRIENDS
Outdoor Activity Book

Based on the picture books by Julia Donaldson
and Axel Scheffler
Activities created by Little Wild Things

CONTENTS

STICK MAN

- Build a Stick Bird Feeder — 10-11
- Make a Twig Tree — 12-13
- Play Fetch — 14-15
- Stick Pencils — 16-17
- Make a Stick Dog Lead — 18-19
- Build a Stick Maze — 20-21

TIDDLER

- Blow Big Bubbles — 24-25
- Build a Rock Pool — 26-27
- Jellyfish Friends — 28-29
- Tiddler's Late — 30-31
- Build a Leaf Fish — 32-33
- Super Stories — 34-35

CONTENTS

THE HIGHWAY RAT

- Foam Cupcakes — 38-39
- Make a Leaf Lantern — 40-41
- Make a Grass Broom — 42-43
- Make Mud Sweets — 44-45
- Create a Collection — 46-47
- Build a Cave — 48-49

THE UGLY FIVE

- Make a Mud Bath — 52-53
- Pouncing Practice — 54-55
- Ugly Bug Hunt — 56-57
- Make a Safari Telescope — 58-59
- Make an Ugly Mud Beast — 60-61
- Care For a Potato Baby — 62-63

Letter from Little Wild Things

Dear adventurers,

Welcome to your very own outdoor activity book!

We are Little Wild Things, a small community organisation whose mission is to get children playing outdoors. We love helping children explore the natural world and giving them new ideas for games and adventures to try outside.

We think spending time outside is really important and so want to make outdoor play as fun and easy as possible. This book is bursting with ideas, inspired by four of our favourite picture books by Julia Donaldson and Axel Scheffler. Use them for a party, in the school holidays, when you're out for a walk, in the sunshine and in the rain!

Get outside and go wild!

Little Wild Things

Hints and Tips

* Ask a grown-up to read through the instructions with you and set up any bits and pieces you need help with.

* Don't worry if you don't have much outside space – plenty of these activities can be done anywhere. Make your way to a park, your nearest playground, or find somewhere to go for a walk.

* Sometimes you'll want to collect things or dig in the ground. Check with your grown-up that you're allowed to before you start!

* Remember to always collect things from the ground rather than picking living flowers or branches.

* Outdoor play can be a little messy so make sure you don't wear your smartest clothes, and always give your hands a good wash after you're finished!

Let's get playing!

STICK MAN

Stick Man lives in the family tree
With his Stick Lady Love and their stick children three.

Stick Man is always being mistaken for an ordinary stick, which gets him into all sorts of trouble!

Sticks are brilliant for games and crafts, so turn the page to discover lots of interesting things you can do with a stick – just be sure to always check it isn't Stick Man or one of his family before you start!

BUILD A STICK BIRD FEEDER

As we know from the story, sticks can be used for all kinds of things. Follow these simple steps to create a delicious sticky snack for the birds in your garden.

ADVENTURE KIT

* A dry stick about the length of your hand and as thick as your thumb
* Some string or wool
* Safety scissors
* Some soft margarine or butter in a bowl
* A plastic knife for spreading
* Some bird seed on a plate

WHAT TO DO

1. Use the scissors to cut a piece of string or wool about as long as your arm.

2. Take the stick and tie the piece of string to the top section of it. Get a grown-up to help you with the knot if it's tricky.

Always ask a grown-up to help when using scissors or a knife.

HINTS AND TIPS
* Make sure the sticks you are using are really dry, or the butter won't stick to them very well.

KEEP ADVENTURING

Find a good spot near your bird feeder to keep watch. See if you can identify any of the birds you see. Small songbirds like blue tits will love eating the seeds off your buttery bird feeder. They often hang upside down to feed like real little acrobats! Ask a grown-up for help to look in a bird book or for an identification chart online.

3. Holding the top part of the stick with the string on, use the knife to spread lots of butter or margarine all over the rest of the stick.

4. Once your stick is well buttered, roll it around on the plate of bird seed so that the butter gets covered in seeds. You can also put the stick down on the plate and sprinkle seeds over it to make sure all the buttery bits are covered.

5. Once your stick is lovely and seedy, it's ready to tie outside as a tasty treat for a bird. Tie it to the branch of a tree, a fence post or the railings on your balcony. How many stick bird feeders will you make?

MAKE A TWIG TREE

Trees are very important to Stick Man, after all, he makes his home in one of them. Have a go at making your own mini tree which you can decorate however you like!

ADVENTURE KIT

* A wooden lolly stick
* Some PVA glue
* A paint brush
* Somewhere you can collect some small twigs

WHAT TO DO

1. First, collect around ten small, straightish twigs to make your tree, making sure they're no thicker than your little finger. Don't worry about how long the twigs are to start with, you can always snap longer twigs into shorter ones.

2. Now prepare your twigs so you can lay out the full shape of the tree before you start gluing. Your finished tree will be the shape of a triangle with long twigs at the bottom and short ones at the top. Snap your twigs to be the right length and lay them out on your lolly stick to make sure they all fit. Your lolly stick is the central trunk of your tree, so your twigs should lie across the trunk with equal amounts on each side. You will probably need about seven twigs.

3. Once you are happy with your twig tree, carefully take the twigs off the lolly stick. Make sure to keep them in the same order with the longest at the bottom and shortest at the top.

KEEP ADVENTURING

Why not decorate your tree? Put some more glue on your tree branches and scrunch up small bits of paper or add little pom-poms to make it really special.

4. Now it is time to glue the twigs onto the lolly stick. Take your paint brush and paint a line of glue along the lolly stick, leaving a little bit at the bottom without glue to be your tree trunk. Use plenty of glue so that your twigs get well and truly stuck down.

5. Take the shortest twig and press it down firmly to the top of the lolly stick. Now take the next, slightly longer twig, and press it down underneath the first. Keep going until you have stuck all the twigs onto the lolly stick.

6. Congratulations! You have made your twig tree! Leave your tree somewhere safe to dry for an hour or two.

HINTS AND TIPS
* Your tree will be a bit wobbly until the glue has dried. Try making your tree on a tray or piece of card so you can move it to a safe place to dry.
* Remember, dry twigs are best for gluing.

PLAY FETCH

"I'll fetch it and drop it, and fetch it – and then I'll drop it and fetch it and drop it again."

Fetch is a great game – just be sure to use an actual stick and not a member of the Stick family! This is perfect to play on a walk.

ADVENTURE KIT

* Some sticks
* A big open space to play
* A grown-up to play with

WHAT TO DO

1. Find a good stick that you want to play with. It's best to choose a reasonably short, thick one that you can easily hold in your hand.

2. Take a good look at your stick and notice its features. Is it very straight or a bit twisty? Is it all one colour, thicker at one end and does it have any holes or interesting marks?

3. Now hand your stick to your grown-up and get your best racing legs ready.

4. Get your grown-up to count down from three and then throw the stick high and far in one direction. Make sure they don't forget to shout, "Fetch!"

5. Once the stick has been thrown, you need to race off after it! When you think you've found it, look at the stick closely to check that it's yours, then pick it up and run straight back to your grown-up.

6. Drop the stick at your grown-up's feet so that you can fetch it all over again!

HINTS AND TIPS

* Make sure your grown-up is careful with where they are throwing and watches out for other families.
* Dogs love this game, but must hold their sticks in their mouths, since their paws aren't much good for carrying. However, sticks don't taste very nice, so be sure to hold yours in your hands!

KEEP ADVENTURING

Are you feeling competitive? Why not ask your grown-up to time you? How quickly can you fetch your stick? Can you beat your own record? Can you pretend to be a dog for this game? Can you do any other tricks? Do you sit when you're asked to, roll over, or beg for a biscuit?

STICK PENCILS

Stick Man might not be a pen, but normal sticks can be great for writing and drawing. Find your perfect stick pencil and get creating!

ADVENTURE KIT

* A shallow tray that your grown-up is happy for you to borrow. An old baking tray works well
* A few handfuls of dry play sand
* A stick to be your pencil

WHAT TO DO

1. Find a place your grown-up is happy for you to get a bit sandy and lay your tray on the ground or somewhere flat.

2. Sprinkle your handfuls of sand into the tray. Give the tray a gentle shake so that the sand spreads out and covers the bottom of the tray with a thin layer. Add more sand if you need to.

3. Now for a test run! Use your stick to draw a circle in the sand. Now try rubbing out your drawing. Give the tray a gentle shake from side to side and watch your circle disappear!

KEEP ADVENTURING

This is great for games like noughts and crosses or hangman! Grab another stick pencil and then you can play with a friend.

HINTS AND TIPS

* The sand and the tray both need to be nice and dry so you can easily shake them and clear away your drawing.
* You can play with this again and again. When you've had enough, you can pop your dry sand in a box so that you can play another day.

4. If your circle hasn't come out clearly, you may have too much sand. A very thin layer of sand works best for this, so take a little sand out before you try again.

5. Once you've got the amount of sand just right, it's time for you to get artistic!

6. Can you draw a smiley face or a wiggly line? Will you write your name? Can you draw a snowman, a dog or Stick Man himself? Keep drawing, shaking, and creating!

MAKE A STICK DOG LEAD

As Stick Man discovered, sticks have so many uses! Why not use one to take your favourite teddy on a walk?

ADVENTURE KIT

* A dog teddy (or another teddy that would like to go for a walk!)
* A stick about as long as your arm
* 50cm of string
* An elastic band
* An old keyring

WHAT TO DO

1. First use the string to make a harness for your dog teddy. Take the piece of string and tie the two ends together to make it into a circle.

2. Hold the circle of string out in both hands. Flip your right hand over so that your circle becomes the shape of a number eight lying on its side. This is your harness, lay it down on the ground.

3. Put the teddy's front legs into the harness. One leg goes into each hoop of the figure eight.

4. Take the edge of each hoop and bring them up over your teddy's back so that they touch. Ask a grown-up to attach the two hoops together using the metal keyring. The string should fit snugly round your teddy's body and back, so you may need to adjust your string so that the harness fits just right.

5. Now thread the elastic band onto the keyring.

6. Next take your stick and wrap the elastic band around one end. Wrap it round two or three times so that it won't slip off. This will be your lead.

KEEP ADVENTURING

If your dog teddy enjoys playing on the lead, why not see if you can come up with an agility course? Can your dog leap over things, balance on a plank seesaw or even jump into a hoop?

7. Your dog teddy is now ready to be walked!

8. Hold your stick lead at the top end and let your dog teddy's legs rest on the floor. Wiggle the lead to get your teddy prancing and dancing about. Hold the lead out in front of you and get your teddy to walk along.

9. Once you've got the hang of walking your dog teddy around, take them on a stroll around the garden or even into the park. Do they enjoy running on the grass, sniffing around the trees or do they stay obediently by your side?

10. Once your teddy is tired, let them have a nice lie down in their bed!

HINTS AND TIPS
* A light stick and a small teddy are good for this - otherwise your dog walking arm can get tired quite quickly! Your teddy might get a bit muddy, so choose one that's happy to go in the wash.
* If you don't have a keyring, a paper clip, a karabiner, or another bit of string will work too.

BUILD A STICK MAZE

Stick Man once got lost, but he managed to find his way back to the family tree. Why not try using sticks to make a maze and challenging friends and family to find their way through?

ADVENTURE KIT

* Lots and lots of sticks of all shapes and sizes!
* A big space to build your maze

WHAT TO DO

1. Find a place to make your maze. A woodland with lots of sticks and a big space to arrange them is perfect!

2. The sticks are the walls of your maze, so start by laying a stick on the ground, then lay a second stick next to the first, leaving enough space between the two for you to walk through. Take another stick and lay it end to end with the first stick, then do the same on the other side. Keep adding sticks in this way to build up your path.

3. After you have made a short path it's time to start building up your maze by making paths which lead in different directions. You can split your path by building a T-junction or a crossroad.

4. Once you have built a few paths, decide which will lead somewhere and which will be dead ends. Lay two sticks across a path to show it's a dead end.

5. Will your maze paths be long and straight, or will they go in a circle? Keep building paths and dead ends until you are happy with your maze.

6. What will be at the end of your maze? Can you collect some conkers or pinecones, or even pile up the family picnic?

7. Now challenge your family to try out your maze. Will they make it through, or will they get lost?

KEEP ADVENTURING

Once you've built your maze, what can you put into it to make it more fun? Could you put some kind of treasure to be collected on the way through, or add in some little piles of stones or nuts that need to be avoided?

HINTS AND TIPS
* It can be difficult to imagine the whole maze at the beginning, but just get started with some paths and you will have a maze before you know it!
* Use things around you to make your maze more exciting. Weave around a tree or stop at a fence.

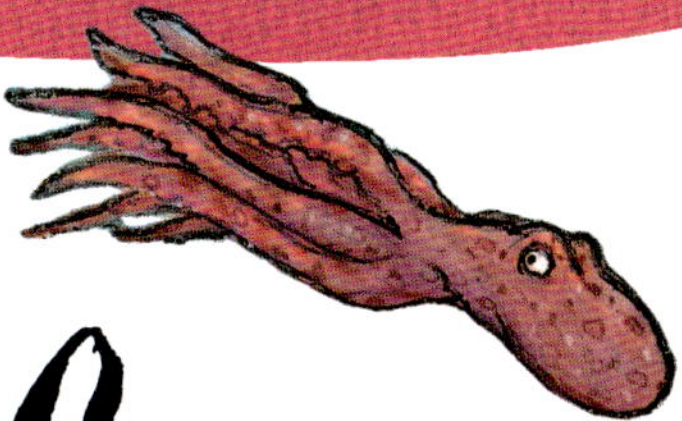

Tiddler

Tiddler was a fish with a big imagination.
He blew small bubbles but he told tall tales.

See if you can be as creative and imaginative as Tiddler!

Turn the page to find out how to build your own rock pool, make some super sea creature friends and get some inspiration for your own tall tales from the world's only story-telling fish!

BLOW BIG BUBBLES

Tiddler might blow small bubbles, but this activity is your chance to create some big and colourful ones!

ADVENTURE KIT

* Three small bowls that can get painty
* Three colours of squeezy paint
* Washing up liquid
* Some water
* A straw
* Some card

WHAT TO DO

1. Squeeze a good blob of paint and the same sized blob of washing up liquid into the bottom of one bowl. Add a small amount of water.

2. Use your straw to blow into the bottom of the bowl. When you blow air into the mixture it should start to bubble up. As you blow more air into the mixture the bubbles should grow bigger and bigger. You get the best bubbles if the end of your straw is completely underneath the mixture.

Remember to always blow rather than suck through your straw, and to take your mouth away from the straw every time you take a big breath in!

3. If you're struggling to get big bubbles, try adding a little more water or a little more washing up liquid. Once you have the right balance of ingredients your bubbles should grow and grow, and may even spill out over the sides!

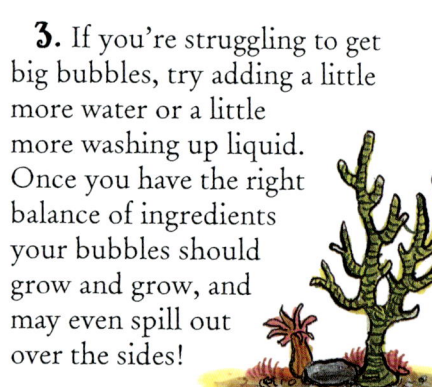

HINTS AND TIPS

* It's a good idea to try and remember which end of the straw you are using to put in the paint mixture and which end you are putting in your mouth.

4. Keep blowing until your colourful bubbles reach the top of the bowl.

5. Now take your piece of card and lay it gently over the bowl. The card will pop the paint bubbles, leaving a lovely colourful pattern behind.

6. Once you've got the hang of things with the first bowl, you can make bubbles of different colours. Use your other paint colours in the other two bowls so that you have three different coloured bubbly bowls.

7. Keep pressing the piece of card over the bubbles to pop them and then blow more bubbles so that you can layer up your picture with lots of colours.

8. Once your card is as colourful and bubbly as you'd like it, put it somewhere safe to dry.

KEEP ADVENTURING

Once your card has fully dried out, you can use pens to add more detail to your picture. Give your bubble outlines eyes, ears, mouths, noses and even teeth!

BUILD A ROCK POOL

Tiddler makes friends with lots of different sea creatures on his adventures. See if you can make a little home for some of them.

ADVENTURE KIT

* A big shallow tray or plastic box that you can put water in
* Some water
* A cup
* Some rocks, gravel or shells
* Grass, moss, leaves and small bits of plant
* Some plastic animals to play in the rock pool

WHAT TO DO

1. Pop your tray or box somewhere outside that is okay to get a little wet.

2. Grab your rocks and shells and place them into the tray to create the rock pool. You could put them in a circle, heap them up to one side or make lots of little piles, whatever you think looks best.

3. Now add your moss, grass and leaves to be the seaweed in your pool. Plants make places for your animals to live and give them plenty to eat. Wedge them under and between the rocks, have them floating in the middle, or even growing up the side.

4. Once all your rocks and plants are in place, use your cup to carefully add water to your pool until it is as deep as you'd like it.

HINTS AND TIPS
* Rocks and pebbles can be heavy so be careful when you're carrying them about and moving them around in your pool, especially when they're wet.
* Sand can be a great thing to put in your pool too, especially if you have a nearby sandpit you can grab a few handfuls from.

KEEP ADVENTURING
What extra things can you think of to make your rock pool super special? Might the animals living there like a leaf boat to float on, a stick slide to splash down or a bridge to cross from one side to the other?

5. Now grab your plastic animals and see how they like the pool you've created! Will they move into a mossy cave, sit on the side to soak up the sun or swim backwards and forwards?

JELLYFISH FRIENDS

Underwater creatures come in lots of shapes and sizes, and jellyfish are some of the most unusual! Can you create a jellyfish of your own?

ADVENTURE KIT

* An old sock
* Safety scissors
* Some double-sided sticky tape
* Some lengths of wool, material and long pieces of grass
* An elastic band
* A handful of hay or some old newspaper
* Sticky googly eyes or a pen to draw eyes with

Always ask a grown-up to help when using scissors.

WHAT TO DO

1. Take your sock and lay it out flat. Use your scissors to cut through the sock below the heel. You can keep the heel end of the sock for another project.

2. Take the toe end of your sock and turn it inside out. Lay this section out flat.

3. Cut a strip of double sided sticky tape and stick it along the bottom edge of your sock.

KEEP ADVENTURING

Can you use different sized socks and create a whole jellyfish family?

Add a little bit of lavender or rosemary when stuffing your jellyfish body to make it smell nice!

4. Peel off the top part of the double-sided tape to leave the sticky section underneath. Press your pieces of wool, strips of material and blades of grass onto the tape with the long lengths dangling down away from the sock. These are going to be your jellyfish tentacles. Make sure all the sticky tape is fully covered.

5. Now carefully turn your sock toes the right way round again.

6. Next take a handful of hay or scrunch up a piece of newspaper and push it into the sock. This will make the body of your jellyfish, so keep adding more until you have a nice round shape.

7. Pop your elastic band over the top of the body and wrap it around the end of the sock so that it holds the hay or newspaper in place while letting the tentacles dangle down.

8. Now add your sticky googly eyes or draw some on with a pen and you have your very own jellyfish friend! Where will you take him first?

TIDDLER'S LATE

Tiddler is often late for class so he has to swim all the way from home super quickly. What obstacles might he meet on his dash to school? Can you create an obstacle course and see how quickly you can make it through?

ADVENTURE KIT

* A stopwatch or timer

* An outside space – a garden, park, woodland or field where you can run about safely

* Some obstacles!

WHAT TO DO

1. First you will need to check that your outdoor space is safe. Have a look around to see that there are no holes in the ground or hidden things you might trip over. You don't need a huge space, just somewhere you can move about either in a circle or a straight line.

2. Now put some obstacles in place. Be creative and use whatever you can find! Can you find something to leap over, something to balance on, something to wiggle around or crawl through? You can use logs, sticks, piles of leaves, rucksacks or even your jumper to make an obstacle. There are lots of different ways to move from one place to another too. You can hop, crawl, sprint, side step or even jump.

HINTS AND TIPS
* There are no rules when it comes to setting up an obstacle course, just think about what you like doing to get you started. Are you a fast runner, can you cartwheel, or do you like climbing and balancing best?

Always check that the items you're using for your obstacle course are safe to move and always ask your grown-up to help.

3. Once you have your course set out, practice by walking through it a few times so you are confident in navigating your obstacles. Then it's time to go against the clock!

4. Ask a friend or grown-up to time you from start to finish. Can you beat your best time? Can you teach the course to a friend? Who can do it fastest? Can you do your course the other way round? Will you make it to class on time?

5. How creative can you be with your course? Could you add in some activities to do on the way round? Can you skip, catch a ball three times in a row, knock a teddy off a chair or put on a hat and scarf and still beat your record?

KEEP ADVENTURING
Parks can be great for this game as they have lots of obstacles in them already. Can you get over the climbing frame, down the slide, round the big tree and back before your grown-up counts to 20? Just be sure to watch out for other adventurers!

BUILD A LEAF FISH

Tiddler meets some fantastically unusual fish on his adventures. Can you create a beautiful and colourful one to inspire one of his stories?

ADVENTURE KIT

* A big piece of flat cardboard
* A pen or pencil
* Lots of leaves of different colours and sizes
* Other natural things to decorate your fish like shells, conkers, stones, moss and grass

WHAT TO DO

1. First, grab your pen or pencil and draw the outline of a fish on your piece of cardboard. Use all the cardboard and make the outline as big as you can. Make sure your fish has a tail, some fins, and an eye. If you're not sure how it should look, ask a grown-up to help you with the drawing or look at the *Tiddler* book for inspiration!

2. Lay your fish outline somewhere flat and gather your leaves. Take one leaf and lay it on the cardboard inside the fish outline, then place another one next to it so that it is slightly overlapping. The leaves will be your fish scales.

KEEP ADVENTURING

Fish scales made of natural items look really cool, but you can also try making your fish scales with toy bricks, coins or recycling for a different look!

HINTS AND TIPS

* If you're super pleased with your creation, you can always glue the leaf scales on to your fish to make a more permanent picture, or you can sweep everything off your outline and put it away to play with another day.

* This is a great activity to try in the autumn when there are lots of leaves falling off the trees that you can easily collect.

3. Keep adding leaves in this way until the main body of your fish is all covered in leaf scales. Your scales could be all different colours, shapes and sizes, or you might choose to make them all look the same. Play around and see what you like the look of best.

4. Once the body of your fish is done, give your fish some leafy fins and fill in the outline of its tail.

5. Finally, use your other natural materials to give your fish an eye and a nice place to swim. Conkers and stones make great eyes and mouths and if you add grass, moss, and shells to the cardboard outside the outline, it will look like your fish is swimming through seaweed in the ocean!

WHAT TO DO

Outdoor stories

We all love stories, but reading a book outside is something extra special. Find a wonderful place to read your favourite story. Under a tree, in some long grass, in a hammock or by a pond. Build a den under a table or on a climbing frame, or a nest of cushions by a sunny wall. Do it on your own or ask someone to read to you. You choose!

Go on a story walk

If you're out walking, why not take a new look at the things around you and see if you can invent a story to explain all the little things you notice. Which animal made those scratches on the trees, who dug that hole, and what is making that noise in the bushes? A dragon, a pixie or maybe Stick Man is around? Where will your imagination take you?

What happens next?

Think about your favourite book and remind yourself of the ending. Have some fun with your friend or parent chatting about what might happen next if the story went on. Will the adventure continue, will life go back to normal or will something unexpected happen?

For example, once Tiddler's story has led him home again, will he take his classmates on a field trip to spot a fishing boat and meet the shoal of anchovies, or will his adventures be made into a blockbuster film?

KEEP ADVENTURING

If you come up with a really good story, why not draw a picture or write it down so you can tell it again and again. You could also tell it to a grown-up who could write it down for you, just like Little Johnny Dory does in *Tiddler*.

The Highway Rat

"Give me your pastries and puddings!
Give me your chocolate and cake!
For I am the Rat of the Highway,
and whatever I want I take."

The Highway Rat goes riding, riding, riding...
so join him out and about for some excellent
adventures. Find yourself some curious keepsakes,
build a cave and make some muddy treats!

FOAM CUPCAKES

Cakes are one of the Highway Rat's favourite treats! Have a go at making these amazing foam creations yourself.

ADVENTURE KIT

* Three bowls that can get messy
* Three colours of food colouring
* Washing up liquid
* Some water
* A whisk or a fork
* A spoon
* Some cupcake cases

Remember, although they might look super tasty, these cupcakes are just for playing and not for eating!

WHAT TO DO

1. Squeeze a small blob of food colouring and a big blob of washing up liquid into the bottom of one bowl. Add a small amount of water.

2. Hold your bowl carefully with one hand and hold the whisk in the other. Use the whisk to mix up the three ingredients.

3. Whisks help get air into a mixture, so move the whisk faster and faster to get in plenty of air until you've made a thick, colourful foam, a bit like shaving foam. This can be tiring for your mixing arm so do ask a grown-up to help!

4. Once you have a foamy bowl of one colour, use your other bowls and other food colourings to make two more bowls of colourful foam.

5. Now grab your cupcake cases and use your spoon to lift foam into a case. Try putting blobs of one colour on top of another or layering a mixture of colours. Use your spoon to make swirls and dents to make your cupcakes really beautiful!

6. Your foam will start to lose bubbles after a few minutes and will shrink down. If it starts going flat in your bowls, just use your whisk to froth it up again.

7. See if you can make yourself a whole tray of cupcakes and put them on display.

HINTS AND TIPS
* Silicone cupcake cases are best for this type of playing, as you can use them again and again!
* However, you can use paper cupcake cases but it's best to double them up or pop them into an old muffin tin.

KEEP ADVENTURING

What finishing flourishes can you give your cakes? Perhaps a bit of bark for a chocolate topping, or some grassy sprinkles? What else can you use your foam for? If you have a toy tea set you can use it to top your pretend hot chocolate or even make a super frothy milkshake!

MAKE A LEAF LANTERN

Once the Highway Rat is defeated, the animals of the highway all celebrate by having a moonlit feast. Have fun making a lantern that would be perfect to light up the celebrations!

ADVENTURE KIT

* A clean glass jar
* PVA glue
* A paint brush
* Somewhere you can collect leaves and flowers
* A battery operated tea light

WHAT TO DO

1. First gather some leaves and flowers to decorate your lantern. Autumn leaves work wonderfully, as they tend to be brilliantly colourful, but leaves at any time of the year will look great.

2. Take your glass jar and cover the outside of it in PVA glue using your paintbrush. Try not to get too much glue on the rim of the jar so you have somewhere to hold it steady.

HINTS AND TIPS

* This can be quite a sticky business! We recommend putting some newspaper down and popping an apron on so you don't get too messy.

* Once your lantern is dry you can always add a second coat of glue on top, to give your delicate decorations an added layer of protection.

3. Now stick the leaves or flowers to the glue all over your jar. You can arrange them however you want. You might want to cover the whole thing, or leave little gaps for the light to shine through.

4. Paint another layer of glue over the top. The glue will look white to start with, but it will dry clear. As well as helping your decorations to stick firmly to your jar, it will give your lantern a lovely shine!

KEEP ADVENTURING

Why not build a cushion and blanket den in your house where you can get cosy and really show off your lantern?

5. Put your lantern somewhere safe overnight so that the glue can dry.

6. Once your glue is set you can pop your tea light inside the jar, wait for it to get dark and then admire your beautiful lantern!

MAKE A GRASS BROOM

The Highway Rat ends his story working in a cake shop, where he spends his time sweeping the cake shop floor. Can you make a grass broom to sweep up any crumbs in your garden?

ADVENTURE KIT

* Somewhere you can cut some long grass
* Safety scissors
* A few elastic bands
* Some string

Always ask a grown-up to help when using scissors.

WHAT TO DO

1. First find some long grass to make your broom. Ideally, you want the long grasses that grow in fields or parks rather than the short stuff that might grow in your garden.

2. Ask your grown-up to help you cut some big handfuls of grass nice and low to the ground so that the pieces are roughly the length of your grown-up's forearm.

3. The bit of grass nearest the ground is slightly thicker than the bit at the top – you'll want to use this part as the handle. Gather your grass together in one hand and use an elastic band around this thick bit to attach it together in one big bundle.

4. Put another elastic band over the first one and then wrap some string round and round the bands to make a place for your hand to go. Tie the string ends nice and tightly to make sure all the pieces of grass are held in securely.

5. Now use your scissors to trim both ends of the broom so that all the pieces of grass are around the same length.

6. Give your broom a good shake to make sure no bits fall out and you are ready to give it a test. Find a bit of patio or a smooth path, hold the broom by the handle and brush the other end over the ground. Does it pick up some bits and pieces?

HINTS AND TIPS

* It can be tricky to hold the grass and attach it together by yourself. Find a grown-up to hold things firmly for you while you make your broom.
* Start with more grass than you think you need as some pieces are bound to fall out.

KEEP ADVENTURING

If you have any nice bits of ribbon or wool, why not add them to your handle to make your broom even more beautiful?

Can you borrow a dustpan to sweep your crumbs into? Then you could even help around the house!

7. Once you've got the hang of it, keep on sweeping – your garden will be free of cake crumbs in no time!

MAKE MUD SWEETS

The Highway Rat loves sweets and chocolates. Can you have a go at making your own pretend sweets?

ADVENTURE KIT

* Somewhere you can collect some mud

* A spoon

* A container that can get muddy

* Some water

* Leaves, flowers, grass, sticks, stones and other natural materials for decoration

Remember, although they might look super tasty, these sweets are just for playing and not for eating!

WHAT TO DO

1. First you will need to gather some mud to build your sweets. The mud will need to be soft but not too wet, so that you can roll it and shape it as you like. Go to your chosen muddy spot and using your spoon, dig out some mud and pop it in to your box. Feel through the mud with your fingers and pick out any stones or roots. Then add a small amount of water to it until it's just right for moulding.

2. Now find somewhere to roll out and decorate your mud sweets. First take a small handful of mud and roll it into a ball. Try making a big ball and a small ball.

3. Once you're used to shaping your mud, it's time to make your sweets! Can you squeeze your mud into a rectangle, or a square? Lay each sweet out carefully so that it doesn't get squashed.

KEEP ADVENTURING

How many different types of sweet treat can you create with your ingredients? Chocolate bars, cakes, lollies and chews – the list is endless!

Can you set up a muddy sweet shop? Set out all your treats beautifully for your customers to look over, and make sure everything has a label and a price tag!

HINTS AND TIPS

* An old baking tray or plate works wonderfully to display your creations.
* If you happen to have any sawdust or dry sand lying around, try rolling your sweet gently in it – it will look a bit like a dusting of sugar.

4. When you've finished rolling and shaping, it's time to decorate! Will you put a petal on top? Dot seeds you have found around the outside, or wrap a long piece of grass round and round a sweet like a ribbon?

5. Keep shaping and decorating until you have a magnificent display!

CREATE A COLLECTION

The animals collect all sorts of things that they carry down the highway. Can you make your own collection of lovely things?

ADVENTURE KIT

* A basket, bucket or pot to put your finds in

WHAT TO DO

1. Decide where you are going to go collecting – this is a great thing to do on a walk, especially in the autumn.

2. Grab your container and start collecting. What will you gather? Can you find a conker or a pine cone? Is the ground covered in beautiful leaves? Can you spot a feather or an interesting pebble?

3. Pop anything you'd like for your collection into your container.

4. Once you have a collection the Highway Rat would be proud of, it's time to take it home and examine it. Spread out your collection on a table or in the garden. How many things did you find? Can you line them up, smallest to biggest? Or put them in colour groups? How many different textures did you discover?

5. Can you think of something cool to do with your collection? Will you display it in your bedroom, use it to make a collage or to build a pattern on the ground?

HINTS AND TIPS

* It's fun to gather lots of different things, but also fun to collect loads of one thing! Try under a horse chestnut tree in the autumn for conkers, an oak tree for acorns or a sweet chestnut tree for chestnuts!

* If your collection is too big to take home, leave it somewhere for someone else to discover!

KEEP ADVENTURING

Once you are good at collecting, ask your grown-up to set you some collecting challenges. Can you find five feathers, something blue, something to keep in your pocket or something to craft with?

Always make sure you're allowed to take what you find for your collection.

BUILD A CAVE

The Highway Rat ventures into a deep dark cave looking for sweets and chocolates. Can you create your own cave to explore?

ADVENTURE KIT

* Blankets or big bits of material
* String or rope
* Sticks
* Logs, trees or garden furniture to build your cave structure

WHAT TO DO

Caves are brilliant places to play, sleep, read and tell stories. Why not try some of these ideas when you build yours?

Build your cave

Your blankets and pieces of material will create the roof and walls of the cave, so start by creating a solid structure to hang these on. You could use long branches and sticks tied together if you are in a woodland or park, or try arranging garden chairs and tables close together if you have them at home. Tight lines of string tied between trees or chairs can help you build your cave roof. Once you have a solid structure, throw your blankets and bits of material over the top.

Make your cave dark

Caves are usually deep and dark so make sure you cover up all the cracks where light could get in. Layering bits of material over each other can also help to stop the light, so keep adjusting your blankets until it's as dark as you can make it.

Add your finishing touches

How will you get into and out of your cave? Will there be a doorway, a small hole or a long dark tunnel? Big cushions leaning together make a great tunnel, or you can try crawling through the legs of a chair. Can you make your cave with a front door and a back door?

What will be inside your cave? Will it be soft and cosy or bare and full of echoes? Will there be particular places to eat, sleep and play?

Play in your cave

Once you've built your cave, how will you play in it? How many children or grown-ups can you fit inside, and does it stay standing when people are crawling through it? Will you chase each other through the cave, have your lunch inside it or just curl up for a snooze?

HINTS AND TIPS
* If it's a wet day, you could use a tarpaulin instead of blankets to see if you can build a cave that will keep you dry!

KEEP ADVENTURING
Once you've made your cave, why not explore it with a torch? Can you make shadows on your cave wall?

The Ugly Five

"We're the ugly five, we're the ugly five.
Everyone flees when they see us arrive."

The Ugly Five live out on the African plain
with many other animals.

Head outdoors and have fun spotting ugly
and lovely creatures alike, and making
some animal friends of your own!

MAKE A MUD BATH

On the African plains it can get very hot! Lots of creatures like to wallow in a mud bath to cool down. Perhaps some of your toys would like that too?

ADVENTURE KIT

* A bin bag or a sheet of plastic to line your mud bath
* Safety scissors
* A bowl that can get muddy
* An old spoon
* A little bit of water
* Some plastic animal toys

Always ask a grown-up to help when using scissors.

WHAT TO DO

1. Find a spot your grown-up is happy for you to dig and play in – a flower bed would be perfect.

2. Take the spoon and dig a shallow hole, about as wide and as deep as half a football – this will be your mud bath! Put the mud you dig out of the hole into your bowl.

3. Line your mud bath with the piece of bin bag or plastic. Take the plastic and press it into the hole so that the whole bottom is covered and the plastic comes out and over the sides. You want a small amount of your plastic sheet to sit on the ground around the edge of your bath, but if it is too big, ask a grown-up to help you trim it down.

4. Cover the plastic on the ground around the edge of your bath with a layer of mud to hold it in place.

KEEP ADVENTURING

Once your animals have cooled off in the mud, they might need a bath in some water to get clean. Can you help? Can any of your toy animals make footprints in the mud around your wallow? Soft mud around puddles, ponds and rivers is a really good place to see animal footprints – take a look next time you're out and about.

5. Now it's time to mix the mud for your bath! Take the bowl of mud, add a little bit of water and give it a mix with your spoon. Will your mud be runny and sloppy like hot chocolate or will it be thick and gloopy like custard? Keep adding water until you have the perfect mixture.

6. Pour the mud from the bowl into your lined bath, and use the spoon to spread it out. If you feel that your bath isn't full enough, just grab some more mud from the flower bed and get mixing and stirring again!

7. When you are happy with your bath, invite your animal toys to come and enjoy a good wallow! Will they be nervous and only want to paddle, or will they be brave and dive straight in?

HINTS AND TIPS
* Be sure to choose toys that can be easily cleaned for this game – plastic ones are best.
* If you don't have a flower bed or a good space to dig, you can always build your mud bath in a plastic tray or bowl.

POUNCING PRACTICE

Many animals have to be expert pouncers as they need to catch creatures for their dinner. Why not practise your pouncing skills and see what you can catch!

ADVENTURE KIT
* A soft toy to be pounced on
* A long piece of string
* A grown-up to play with

WHAT TO DO

1. Once you have chosen a toy that is happy to play, grab your piece of string and ask your grown-up to help tie one end around your toy. It's usually best to tie the string around the toy's tummy so that it doesn't fall off when you start pouncing!

2. Place your toy on the floor and ask your grown-up to hold the end of the string. Now your grown-up should pull on the string to make the toy move around. Give them a few tries to get the hang of it. Will they make the toy wiggle, jump, or dash away?

3. Time for pouncing practice! Crouch down low, watch closely and when you think the time is right, pounce by jumping forward and trying to catch the toy in your hands. Did you manage, or did your grown-up move it away too quickly?

4. Keep working on your technique until you've perfected your pounce. How stealthy can you be? How quickly can you move? Would you make a fearsome leopard or a ferocious lion?

HINTS AND TIPS

* Large toys are usually easier to catch, so maybe start with a big toy and then try a smaller one as your pouncing skills improve.

* A thick piece of string or rope will be easier for your grown-up to hold and less likely to snap when you pounce!

KEEP ADVENTURING

Can you take a turn holding the string and moving the toy around for your grown-up to pounce on?

Try taking the game to the park — more space makes your toy harder to catch!

UGLY BUG HUNT

Bugs aren't really ugly, they're marvellous! But they often have some interesting features, just like the animals in the story. Take a close look around you to see what you can discover.

ADVENTURE KIT

* A bucket or container to keep your bugs in
* An old spoon

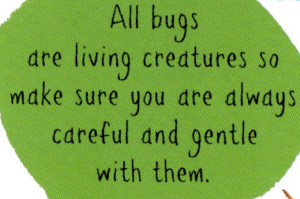

All bugs are living creatures so make sure you are always careful and gentle with them.

WHAT TO DO

1. First decide on where you're going to go on your ugly bug hunt. Have you got a garden you can explore? Could you and your grown-up go for a walk or pop to the park?

2. Once you've found a good spot, think about where you'll look. Lots of bugs live in dark, damp places like underneath logs, in piles of dead leaves or on the underside of plants. Get down on your hands and knees and start searching.

3. Once you have spotted your first bug, take your bucket and gently scoop the creature into it using the spoon.

4. Now take a look! Is it ugly? Is it fascinating? How many legs does it have? Does it have eyes or wings? What colour is it? Does it have horns or pincers or a tail?

KEEP ADVENTURING

A magnifying glass is a great bit of kit for looking at bugs as it makes small things look bigger. Make sure you dig yours out if you have one.

Do you have a book that can help you identify your finds? What are their real names?

5. Can you make up a name for your bug based on how it looks and moves? What about a slimy squiggler, a squelchy squeeze-ball, or even a leggy wanderer?

6. Once you have taken a good look, it is time to carefully release your bug back where you found it.

7. Keep hunting – can you find five different bugs? Would you call them your Ugly Five, or give them a different name?

HINTS AND TIPS

* It's best not to try and catch flying bugs as their wings are really delicate and can be easily damaged.

* Remember that if you're lifting logs or leaves to find your bugs, always put things back just as you found them.

MAKE A SAFARI TELESCOPE

A safari is a trip out to look for wild animals. Whether you are looking for warthogs in Africa or squirrels in the park, a telescope will help you spot all sorts. Can you make your own to see which animals are living near you?

ADVENTURE KIT

* A solid cardboard tube, no longer than 30cm

* A roll of thick tape (Gaffer tape or similar)

* Safety scissors

Always ask a grown-up to help when using scissors.

WHAT TO DO

1. Take your cardboard tube and the roll of tape. Unroll the tape and stick it all around the top of your tube so that around a centimetre of tape pokes out over the edge.

2. You want the entire tube to be covered, so without cutting the tape, keep unrolling it and wrapping it around the tube, working downwards as you go. Make sure that each new layer of tape overlaps with the one before it. It's quite tricky to hold the tube and wrap the tape around at the same time, so ask your grown-up for help.

3. Once you get to the bottom of your tube, keep wrapping the tape around so that there is a centimetre of tape poking out at the bottom, just as there is at the top.

4. Now cut the tape and put the roll to one side.

HINTS AND TIPS
* If it's tricky to close just one eye at a time, cover the eye not using the telescope with your free hand.
* A toilet or kitchen roll tube with masking tape will also work for this, but might not last quite as long.

5. Use the scissors to make three small cuts in the circle of tape poking over the top of your tube. Fold the three pieces of tape inside the tube and press them down so that they stick.

6. Do the same at the bottom of your tube so that the ends are nice and neat.

7. Use your hands to press the tape down all along the length of the telescope to make sure the tape is good and stuck. Your telescope is complete!

8. Now practise using your telescope. Hold it up to one eye and close your other eye while you look though to see what you can see.

9. It's time to take your telescope out on a safari! What can you spot in your park or garden? Can you spy any birds out of the window?

KEEP ADVENTURING
Can your grown-up set up a safari for you? They could put some animal teddies around the garden for you to spot!

MAKE AN UGLY MUD BEAST

The Ugly Five are covered in warts and spots, hairs and wrinkles. Animals have all sorts of fascinating features which help them survive and thrive. Can you create an ugly mud beast of your very own?

ADVENTURE KIT

* Some thick clay-type mud that you can mould in your hands

* A little water

* Something to build your mud beast on — an old baking tray or a plastic plate

* Some natural materials — such as stones, twigs, leaves, grass or petals

WHAT TO DO

1. First check your mud is right for creating a mud beast and take out any chunky bits of wood or stone. The kind of mud you need should be squashy enough for you to mould easily in your hands, but not too sticky, and not so dry it falls apart when you let go. Add water or more mud to get the right mixture.

2. Now put a handful of mud onto your tray and start shaping it. First decide on your beast's body. Will it be big and round or long and skinny? Then your beast needs a head, or maybe two! Make sure to gently squash the head on firmly so it doesn't fall off.

3. Then add some more detail. Will your beast have skinny twig legs, a big stone beak, tatty leaf wings or a bristly grass tail?

4. What other fascinating features might your ugly beast have? Camouflaging spots, stinging prickles, poisonous warts or strong tusks? What will best help your beast survive and find food?

5. Once your beast is complete, it's time to give them a name and release them into the wild. Would they like to guard your front door, hang out by the flower bed or take in the sights at the park? Is your mud beast ugly or is it really quite lovely?

HINTS AND TIPS
* If your beast doesn't look quite as you wanted it to, don't worry, you can always squish it up and start again.
* An old towel is helpful in this activity to give your hands a quick wipe on once you've done your main bit of sculpting.

KEEP ADVENTURING
How many ugly mud beasts can you make? Could you make your own Ugly Five?
If you're doing this with some friends, could you make a whole safari of ugly mud beasts?

CARE FOR A POTATO BABY

The Ugly Five are excellent parents. How good are you at caring for a potato baby?

ADVENTURE KIT

* A potato
* A pen

If you don't have a potato, apples and carrots make good babies too!

WHAT TO DO

Create your baby by drawing a face on your potato. Will your baby be happy and smiley, will they be sleepy, or will they be crying? You need to look after your baby very carefully, so decide what you'd like to do first. Here are a few ideas to try!

Feed your baby

Your potato baby will need some food. What delicious things can you find outside to offer them? Would they like a juicy blade of grass, a petal salad or some stick crisps? Babies can be a bit fussy though, so you may need a selection of snacks!

Make your baby a swing

Potato babies love to swing! You could push your baby on a big swing at the park or you could make a mini one for them to enjoy at home. An old face mask makes a great swing for a potato baby!

Play with your baby

Might they like a go on the slide, would they like to play with your toys, or perhaps they would just like to snuggle up for a story?

Give your baby a bath

Pour some water into an old ice cream tub and let your potato baby have a splash about. You could even ask to put a squeeze or two of bubble bath in if you have some. Just remember to keep your baby's face above the water so they don't get foam in their mouth!

Put your baby to bed

Potato babies need to sleep a lot. Where could yours snuggle up? Is there a soft bit of grass you could find for them, some moss or a pile of leaves?